W9-BRM-706

Show Me You Love Me

This book has been purchased by:

Harrison County Safe & Drug Free
School Funds

304-326-7300

Show Me You Love Me

A Parent's Fun Guide to Teaching Children They are Valuable

Tara Koerber

♥

Beatify Books
Kingmont, WV

Copyright © 2006 by Tara Koerber
Cover design © 2006 by Beatify Books

All rights reserved. This book, or parts thereof, may not be reproduced in any form without written permission from the publisher; exceptions are made for brief excerpts used in published reviews.

Published by:
Beatify Books
P.O. Box 140
Kingmont, WV 26578-0140
Beatifybooks.com

ISBN 0975476009
ISBN 13: 9780975476000
Library of Congress Control Number: 2005908170

To my beautiful children,
I am so blessed to have you in my life.
I only hope that I make you feel half as special as you really are.
Each one of you is a priceless treasure and I am the luckiest woman in the world to get to hold you.
I love you infinity, infinity, infinity....

To Mrs. Judy Cook,
You have touched my son's life in the most profound way. I love the look in his eyes when he describes how lovable you are. You are irreplaceable. Thank you.

To Mrs. Joyce Evans,
The room lights up whenever you look at a child. You find something wonderful to praise in each student. Your energy, enthusiasm, and creativity are contagious! Thank you.

To Mrs. Kerr,
You make school a warm and nurturing place to be. You are first class. We are blessed to have found your school. Thank you.

Contents

Introduction

It appears that once a person hits the age of twenty-one, the years begin to fast forward. Through this whirling momentum our children escape and fly by us. We are caught in this whirlwind of time being pulled in every direction by work, bills, and the stressors of life. When we look away, just for an instant, our children are grown and we have missed their childhood.

What can we do to juggle these stressors more effectively so that we may have more time with our children? Everyday we can create the illusion of stopping time, even if just for a few moments. We have the power to help create incredible moments for our children. "Moments" that as an adult they will have compiled into memories from childhood. They are like brief snapshots in a photo album. They are glimpses at moments that were special or meaningful. Choose an item from this book to try right now! Life is too short.

The Daily Checklist

☐ **Tell my child one thing about him/her that I am grateful for today.**

☐ **Do one loving act to demonstrate how very much I care.**

☐ **Say I love you.**

Reflect on the magical memories you have created and will continue to create.

"Where there is great love, there are always miracles."
                                    -Willa Cather

1. Monday: Mommy Airlines ✈

One day my son was playing in the backyard when an airplane flew right by him and landed on the ground next to him. He looked all around and no one was to be seen. He proceeded to pick up his *paper* airplane and inspect it. Inside he found a message that read, " I ♡ U-Mom."

Do not wait! Grab a piece of paper now and fold it to make a paper airplane. On both sides of the wings write Mommy Airlines. Inside include a cute message. You could even include a message to meet you inside for a game of Monopoly!

2. Tuesday: Car Seat Surprises ☺

Every time I pick up my children from school, I leave a sweet surprise for them to find when they get into the car. It is usually a favorite snack because they are ravenous after school. Sometimes I place a cute note or present onto their seats. They never know what it will be ahead of time and it makes the drive home fun.

♡♡♡♡♡
♡♡♡

3. Wednesday: Spelling Fun

Is it really possible to transform the monotonous task of practicing spelling words into a fun and exciting time spent together? It can be with a little creativity! Purchase a package of dry erase markers and let your child wonder each evening where he/she will be writing the evening's spelling list. Many surfaces of appliances are fully erasable. (Test it out first.) We use the dishwasher, mirrors, windows, and the refrigerator. Your child will be utterly surprised to get to write on these "forbidden" objects. Make sure you explain to only use this type of dry erase marker and to only write on objects Mommy has approved!

4. Thursday: Papa Please Get Me the Moon ☆

Read the story *Papa Please Get Me the Moon* and then scoop your child up, (wrapped in a blanket), and sneak out into the night to find the moon together. Your child may light up as brightly as the moon!

5. Friday: Dance Party ♫

Pick some of your child's favorite music. Turn it up real loud and invite your child to have a dance party. "Play Dates" love this type of party as well!

"There are no seven wonders of the world in the eyes of a child. There are seven million."

-Walt Streightiff

♯ ♯ ♯ ♯ ♯ ♯ ♯ ♯ ♯ ♯ ♯ ♯ ♯

6. Saturday: Breakfast in Bed ✾

Everyone loves to feel like a prince or princess once in a while. Show your child how special he/she is by bringing him/her breakfast in bed.

7. Sunday: Silly Sandwich ☻

When you make your child's sandwich today make it into a fun shape. We use cookie cutters to make witches hats, pumpkins, and ghosts.

♡♡♡♡♡♡♡♡♡♡

8. Monday: The Deluxe Bubble Bath ○

Any moment can be made fun and exciting with a fresh perspective. Tell your child that tonight he/she is not getting an ordinary bath but "The Deluxe Bubble Bath". He/She will be eager with anticipation wondering what exactly this "Deluxe Bubble Bath" entails. My children even request it by name all the time now. I simply run a bubble bath filled with warm vanilla sugar scent, light a vanilla candle (make sure it is out of reach of little ones) and leave a warm fresh towel. When the bath is over, I let my child blow out the candle. It is as simple as this and I hear frequently, "Please, please mom can I have a Deluxe Bubble Bath tonight?" I think everyone deserves to be pampered occasionally.

"There's nothing that can help you understand your beliefs more than trying to explain them to an inquisitive child."

-Frank A. Clark

◇◇◇◇◇◇◇

9. Tuesday: Pumpkin Patch

✂

Go to the pumpkin patch together to select the perfect pumpkins for decorating. Parents, make sure to decorate one as well. Kids like to see you having fun! Take lots of pictures of the finished products.

10. Wednesday: Lunchbox Notes ✉

When you pack your child's lunch, leave a surprise lunchbox note for him/her to discover at school. It can have a funny joke inside, something your child has done that has made you proud, or how much you enjoyed spending time with him/her.

11. Thursday: Magic Sleeping Spray
✪

Should the occasion arise that your child is having difficulty falling asleep, tell him/her that you have just the thing to put him/her deeply in slumber. Have on hand a bottle of lavender pillow spray. It is a clear spray that they sell at Bath and Body Works. You spray it onto your pillow and the relaxing scent of lavender lulls you to sleep. The key here is that you call it *"magic spray"*. It might even be water in a small spritzer bottle. Spritz the pillow and tell your child to count sheep, cows, giraffes, whatever you fancy.

☺☺☺

"Cleaning your house while your kids are still growing up is like shoveling the walk before it stops snowing."

-Phyllis Diller

✿✿✿✿✿✿✿
✿✿

12. Friday: Halloween Decorations

This doesn't have to be expensive. Go to the Dollar Store and let each of your children pick out some Halloween decorations. Let each child use his/her own supplies to decorate your home. It does not matter how it looks; what is important is instilling a sense of accomplishment and pride. "I did it!"

Have you hugged your child today?

13. Saturday: Green Eggs and Ham ❣

Read the story *Green Eggs and Ham* aloud to your children and then emerge from the kitchen with some for them to try! It is amazing what a little green food coloring can do!

14. Sunday: Story Time ☺

When you put your children to bed tonight, take turns telling stories. Use your children as the main character in an exciting adventure with castles and dragons! Kids look forward to their turn telling stories too!

"Don't just tell your child you love him-show him."

-Coley Lamprecht

♥ ♥ ♥ ♥ ♥

15. Monday: Bob for Apples
●

Want your children to eat more fruit?
Try this activity after school and you
will be surprised how eager your
children will be to eat some fruit! Simply
fill a bucket with some water and apples.
Your child must then try to pick up the
apple using *only* his/her mouth!

16. Tuesday: Collect Leaves Together ☼

Inform your children that you are going
on a hunt. Grab some plastic bags and
head out the door. Once you are outside,
begin your leaf hunt seeing how many
different types of leaves that you can
find.

"The only thing worth stealing is a kiss from a sleeping child."

-Joe

♡♡♡♡♡♡♡♡♡

17. Wednesday: Backyard Kickball

○

Invite your children outside for a game of kickball. Invite the neighborhood children as well. Kids really love when their parents play with them. You are never too old to play!

18.Thursday: Sidewalk Chalk Greeting

✎

Welcome your child home with a greeting on the sidewalk, or driveway. "Great job on your test," or "Excellent touchdown," will boost your child's self-esteem and brighten the day.

"Children seldom misquote. In fact, they usually repeat word for word what you shouldn't have said."
                    -Author unknown

☺☺☺☺☺

19. Thursday: Incoming
☺

Buy a package of water balloons and have a war with your child and the neighborhood kids.

20. Friday: Wear a T- Shirt
✍

Using fabric paint you can make a T-shirt that says, "Proud parent of _____." You can also use your computer and buy an appliqué and iron your declaration onto a t-shirt.

Children are treasures!

Make everyday special.

21. Saturday: The Wall of Recognition

In our house the designated wall is in the kitchen. I hang all my children's artwork, awards, and important papers here. I keep them up until the wall gets full and then I start over again.

♥ ♥ ♥ ♥ ♥ ♥

22. Sunday: The Color Game

⧖

Use food coloring and a clear container of water. Kids can learn that 2 drops of blue and 2 drops of red will create purple. Red and yellow make orange, etc. Pretend that you are mad scientists making some crazy potion! You can even wear lab coats.

23. Monday: Fireflies ✳

On a warm summer evening grab a jar and poke holes in the lid. Have fun catching fireflies together and setting them free!

"We worry about what a child will become tomorrow, yet we forget that he is someone today."

-Stacia Tauscher

◇◇◇◇◇
◇

24. Tuesday: Treasure Hunt
❀

If your child can read, write out simple clues that lead up to a small prize like a favorite candy bar. If your child cannot read yet, draw pictures such as the refrigerator, the bed, and the kitchen table that lead to a hidden treasure!

25. Wednesday: Bathroom Message
✐

When your child gets up in the morning to get ready for school, let him/her discover a secret message. Write with soap on the mirror, "You are a great kid!"

"A child is not a vase to be filled,
but a fire to be lit."

-Rabelais

26. Thursday: Picnic
❁

If the weather is nice, have a surprise picnic outdoors. If the weather is cold and rainy, have a cozy picnic inside!

27. Saturday: Scary Movie Night
☆

Pretend it is Halloween evening and rent some scary movies and eat popcorn until it gets very late! We love the movie Gremlins! (This idea is for older kids and not to be used if your child is prone to nightmares.)

"There is no better exercise for the soul than reaching down and lifting a child close to your heart."
             -Krystyna Elizabeth Bublick

28. Sunday: Pet Store Fun
☺

Have an outing at the pet store. Play with all the animals for hours. Kids love the pet store!

29. Monday: Play Backyard Football
☼

Are you ready for some football? Take time out of your busy schedule just to play one game!

"You can learn many things from children. How much patience you have, for instance."

-Franklin P Jones

30.Tuesday: The Smelling Game

❀

Blindfold your child and have him/her guess what he/she smells. I use items such as peanut butter, grape jelly, cinnamon, vanilla extract, maple syrup, etc. It is a fun and exciting game for little ones!

31.Wednesday: Under the Pillow ✉

Leave your child a small gift under his/her pillow for no reason at all. It can be a card, a new pencil, or a small chocolate. Something small can generate an amazing smile.

Actions speak louder than words!

32. Thursday: Car Art

Use window markers or dry erase markers to leave a message on the window your child looks out of.

Pick an idea right now and enjoy the smile it produces!!!

33. Friday: Celestial Ceiling
☆

Hang glow in the dark stars from the ceiling as a surprise for your child. Do not tell him/her that the stars are there and when you shut off the light in the evening the ceiling will awe him/her!

34. Saturday: Write a Story Starring Your Child
✍

Write an exciting adventure starring your child. He/She will have fun making the illustrations with you for the story. In the end you will have "our book" that you made together to snuggle up and read together.

35. Sunday: Expedition
☞

Go exploring in the woods. Chart uncharted territory.

36. Monday: Balloons
♥

For no reason at all bring your child home a bouquet of balloons. Tell him/her how lucky you are to have him/her in your life.

◆ ◆ ◆ ◆ ◆ ◆ ◆

"A child can ask questions that a wise man cannot answer."
                    -Author Unknown

❀❀❀❀❀❀

37. Tuesday: Surprise Dinner

☺

Surprise your child by taking him/her out to eat at a Japanese Steakhouse. Children usually love to watch the chef put on a show as the meal is being cooked!

38. Wednesday: The Touching Game

✌

This idea is similar to the smelling game. Get a pillowcase and fill it with various items for your child to reach in and guess. Choose lots of different textures to make things interesting!

❀❀❀❀❀❀❀

39. Thursday: Dandelion
❀

Pick a white dandelion and present it to your child with instructions to blow and make a wish.

40. Friday: Cheesy Message
🖊

Deliver your child a message written with the spray cheese. Use crackers and spell out the letters of your child's name. You can also write "I ♡ U," draw shapes or silly pictures.

"Children need love, especially when they do not deserve it."
                              -Harold Hulbert

41. Saturday: Indoor Construction Site
✓

Saturday is the perfect day to set up your own construction zone. Lay a large plastic trash bag on the floor to enable easy cleanup. Use a package of chocolate cake for "the dirt." Grab a few toy construction vehicles and you are ready to dig!

42. Sunday: Candy Wall ☺

Surprise your child with an entire wall covered with his/her favorite treat. I taped Kit-Kats all over our wall to surprise my son. You can use fruit roll-ups or healthy treats if you prefer. The smile when he came home was priceless!

"Children are one third of our population and all of our future."
-Select Panel for the Promotion of Child Health,1981

⇒⇒⇒⇒⇒

43. Monday: Mirror Mirror on the Wall

❁

Write a message on the mirror using dry erase markers or soap. First draw a huge heart so that when your child looks in the mirror his/her face will appear in the heart. On the top of the mirror write the message, "Mirror Mirror on the wall, who is the most loved of all?" On the bottom write: "You are!"

Give a great big hug! ☺

44. Tuesday: Happy Kid Day

☺

What better day to celebrate than an ordinary Tuesday? Make this one extra special by baking a cake together to celebrate "Happy Kid Day." Sing together and blow out the candles!

45. Wednesday: Puzzle Time

☺

Do a puzzle with your child today. It just takes a few minutes to show him/her you care!

"Children are the living messages
we send to a time we will not see."
-John W. Whitehead

☆☆☆☆☆☆☆

46. Thursday: Deluxe Milkshakes

☺

Today make milkshakes and be sure to top them with whipped cream and a cherry! Presentation and attitude are everything. Anything can be transformed with the right words and lots of love. Think lima beans are boring? Bet you haven't tried Mom's magic beans that make you invisible. Oh no, where has little Johnny gone?

♥ ♥ ♥

47.Friday: The Tasting Game
☺

This is another variation of the game where the child is blindfolded and the parent collects items for the child to correctly guess. Pick some of your child's favorite treats to taste. Use different temperatures and textures to make a fun learning experience. Ice cream, watermelon, chocolate pudding, Jell-O, are great items to try. Have fun!

◆ ◆ ◆ ◆

"What is a home without children?
Quiet."

-Henny Youngman

48. Saturday: Slapjack
☺

Tonight play a game of slapjack with your child. Use an ordinary deck of cards and flip them over one by one until you see a Jack. The first person to slap the Jack with their hand will win the stack of cards. Whoever wins the most cards wins the game!

49. Sunday: More Spelling Fun
✎

Clear off the kitchen table. Cover a portion of it in shaving cream. Let your child trace spelling words in the cream! Substitute whip cream if a shaving cream allergy exists!

50. Monday: Roast Marshmallows
♥

One evening we lost power and the kids were scared. I decided we should roast mini-marshmallows over our campfire (a small candle). We told stories and everyone forgot about being scared . We used extra long toothpicks for our marshmallows. The kids had so much fun they were disappointed when the electricity was restored. Now they request our mini-campfire all the time. Make sure you use strict supervision and remind your children never to play with fire.

We have the power to create lasting memories for our children. Try an idea now!

"Anyone who thinks the art of conversation is dead ought to tell a child to go to bed."

-Robert Gallagher

❣❣❣❣❣❣❣❣❣❣❣

51. Tuesday: Bath Fizz
☺

Sometimes kids are reluctant to stop playing and take a bath. Now there are all kinds of products that make bath time exceptionally fun. There are tablets that you can plop in that fizz and make the water turn wonderful colors. Check your drugstore!

52. Wednesday: Build a Fort
♡

Build a fort using pillows, sofa cushions, and blankets . Make it large enough for you to fit inside with your child. You can even pretend there are monsters outside.

53.Thursday: Play Restaurant
☺

Children like to pretend to be the chef of his/her own restaurant. Order something simple from the kitchen and let your child prepare it for you!

54. Friday: Flying Flapjacks
✈

Watch the *Father Bear's Famous Flying Flapjack* episode of *Little Bear's Family Tales* together. When you are finished make your own batch of flying flapjacks together!

"Any kid will run any errand for you if you ask at bedtime."
                              -Red Skelton

✧✧✧✧✧✧✧✧✧✧✧✧✧✧✧✧✧✧✧✧✧✧✧
✧✧✧✧✧✧

55. Saturday: Play School

Pretend to be the student and your child can be the teacher. Let your child teach you something he/she has learned this week at school. It will be fun for your child to get to boss you around for a change!

56. Sunday: Take a Walk

After dinner tonight take a walk with your child. Listen to the sounds of nature. Count how many birds or squirrels you can find.

"Memory is a child walking along the seashore. You never can tell what small pebble it will pick up and store away among its treasured things."

-Pierce Harris

57. Monday: Game Night♟

Start a family game night! After dinner tonight play a game of UNO, Scrabble, Monopoly, or Don't Break the Ice!

58. Tuesday: More Spelling Fun

When you practice spelling words today do them outside on the sidewalk or on the driveway. Using sidewalk chalk will transform what might have been a mundane homework assignment!

"Children are travelers in an unknown land and we are their guides."

-Robert Fisher

59. Wednesday: Bake Cookies 🍽

This is a classic idea that is sure to generate warm fuzzies for a lifetime. Your child will have fun being your assistant chef, measuring, cracking eggs, stirring, and plopping cookie dough on the pan (perhaps in silly shapes or the letters of your child's name). Be creative, have a blast, and enjoy the scent of freshly baked cookies wafting through your home.

♥ ♥ ♥ ♥ ♥ ♥

60.Thursday: Hide 'N' Seek

After school today clear 20 minutes from your schedule to play a classic game of Hide 'N' Seek. "Ready or not here I come!"

61. Friday: Album Time

Tonight snuggle up and look at old family albums together. Ask your child to share some of his/her favorite memories!

"Children are our most valuable resource."
-Herbert Hoover

62. Saturday: Obstacle Course ⍋

Little boys especially love this idea! Take a pile of sofa cushions or bed pillows and pile them onto the floor so that they can be jumped onto. Plan out a course that involves rescuing a beloved stuffed animal or baby doll. Use blankets to create lava or water. You can even use a stopwatch to record the quickest time!

63. Sunday: Puppet Show 🗫

Stage a small puppet show with your child. You can use the puppets to role-play and work out solutions to problems that may be bothering him/her.

❤ ❤ ❤ ❤ ❤

64. Monday: Vocabulary Charades 🎬

Use your child's vocabulary list to play a game of charades. Write the words down onto tiny slips of paper and have your child pick them out of a hat to act out.

65. Tuesday: Favorite Color Day ♥

Celebrate your child's favorite color throughout an entire day! For example, if his/her favorite color is pink, serve some pink milk with pink flowers. Write little notes that state what a great kid he/she is on pink paper. Wear pink clothes and cook pink pancakes for dinner!

"A mother's children are portraits
of herself."

-Anonymous

♥ ♥ ♥ ♥ ♥ ♥ ♥ ♥ ♥ ♥ ♥

66. Wednesday: Color Together 🖼

Enjoy a quiet evening coloring together. Try and get as absorbed into the drawing as you would have when you were younger. Surprise your child by framing the pictures and hanging them side-by-side.

67. Thursday: Hot Cocoa 🌙

Share a cup of hot cocoa with your child while reading a couple of stories together. If you feel ambitious, construct a tent and read the stories by flashlight.

♥ ♥ ♥ ♥

"Never fear spoiling children by making them too happy. Happiness is the atmosphere in which all good affections grow."

-Thomas Bray

68. Friday: The Special Journal 🗓️

Start keeping a journal that you share with your child. He/She can write notes to you in it about any feelings, thoughts, or problems that he/she may have. Sometimes it is easier to write about things than it is to talk about them. You can write back offering your support and encouragement. You may wish to include jokes, reasons you are proud of him/her, and things you are excited about.

❤ ❤ ❤ ❤

69. Saturday: Family Award Dinner 🏆

Tonight you may want to hold a special family awards dinner. Be sure to give out invitations to each person attending. Cook a favorite dish loved by every family member. Play music and hand out award certificates. Use the awards to remind each person that he/she is a valuable member of the family!

70. Sunday: Indoor Basketball ●

Use crumpled up balls of paper and waste paper baskets to play a 20-minute game of basketball. You can use masking tape to make shooting lines.

"All children are artists. The problem is how to remain an artist once he grows up."

-Pablo Picasso

WINTER IDEAS

71. Monday: Color the Snow ❄

Use an empty spray container and fill it with water and food coloring. You and your child can make pretty pictures in the snow. Surprise your child with an "I love you" written in the snow!

72. Tuesday: Build a Snow Family 👪

Make a snowman to represent each member of your family. Let your child decorate them! Take lots of pictures!

73. Wednesday: The Foot Bath 🛋

Fill a large bowl with warm water. Let your child soak his feet inside for several minutes. Gently dry them with a warm towel, apply lotion, don warm fuzzy socks! You would be amazed at how relaxing this can be.

74. Thursday: Sticky Surprise 📚

Secretly hide a sticky note inside one of your child's notebooks the evening before school. Your child will be so surprised to find the note the next day. It is sure to elicit a smile!

"Bitter are the tears of a child:
Sweeten them.
Deep are the thoughts of a child:
Quiet them.
Sharp is the grief of a child: Take
it from him.
Soft is the heart of a child: Do not
harden it."
                    -Pamela Glenconner

75. Friday: Runaway Together

Read *The Runaway Bunny* together. Discuss the depth of a parent's love for their child. Tell him/her how lucky you are to have him/her! Then pack a small backpack and "runaway" together. Bring trail mix and drinks. Flip a coin at each intersection. Heads could mean to turn right and tails could mean to turn left. See where you end up! It's an adventure. Simply enjoy being together, walking, and the beauty of nature.

♥ ♥ ♥ ♥ ♥ ♥ ♥

76. Saturday: Play Movie Theater ▢

Let your kids "sell" tickets to one of the family's favorite home videos. Use fake money and pretend ticket stubs. You can make popcorn and snuggle up together. One of our favorite movies is *The Incredibles*.

77. Sunday: Pillowcase Notes 🛏

Leave a sweet note under your child's pillow for him/her to find upon settling in.

❤ ❤ ❤ ❤ ❤

"All kids are gifted; some just open their packages earlier than others."
                                                              -Michael Carr

★ ★ ★ ★ ★ ★ ★ ★

78. Monday: Swing 📖

Go to the playground with your child today. Vow to participate for at least 20 minutes. Swing with your child. Play hide 'n' seek or tag if you are able. Not only will you be getting great exercise your child will light up before your eyes!

79. Tuesday: Signs ✹

Hang Banners or signs around the house for your child to find. Have one stating that he/she is the greatest kid!

❤❤❤❤❤❤❤

"The question for the child is not
"Do I want to be good?" but
"Whom do I want to be like?"
                    -Bruno Bettelheim

♥ ♥ ♥ ♥ ♥ ♥ ♥ ♥

80. Wednesday: Magic Carpet ★

If there are 2 adults able to put your child to bed this evening, then carry him/her off to dreamland with a magic carpet ride. Simply have each adult hold an end of the carpet with the child sitting on top of a small rug or blanket.

81. Thursday: Back Scratcher ⟡

Tonight gently scratch your child's back until he/she falls asleep. You can even draw pictures and tell a story. To reinforce the alphabet you can trace the letters and have your child guess them!

82. Friday: Art Outing

Visit an art museum together. Find a piece that interests your child. Research the artist together.

83. Saturday: Fantasy Questions ?

At bedtime tonight lie next to your child in the dark and ask open-ended questions. If you found a thousand dollars what would you do with it? If you could be an animal, what kind would you be and why? What do you suppose a cat thinks about all day?

"Of all nature's gifts to the human race, what is sweeter to a man than his children?"

-Marcus Tullius Cicero

84. Sunday: Zoo 🖋

Visit the zoo together. Sit by his/her favorite animals and draw them together.

85. Monday: Blanket Swing /⊓\

If there are 2 adults available have each hold the end of a sturdy blanket. Have your child lie in the middle and close the blanket around him/her. Gently swing your child back and forth. He/She will *NEVER* want to stop!

86. Tuesday: Start a Collection 🕮

Find out what interests your child and begin a collection today. It could be leaves or dried up bugs or even pencils!

87. Wednesday: Piggyback Rides

Give your child a piggyback ride to and from the car today. Give rides to dinner, to the bathtub, and to bed tonight. Be prepared for giggles and squeals of delight!

💗💗💗💗💗💗

"Don't worry that children never listen to you. Worry that they are always watching you."
                                    -Robert Fulghum

👁 👁 👁 👁 👁

88. Thursday: Disguises

Dress up in disguises with your child and walk around your neighborhood together. See if anyone recognizes you.

89. Friday: Fishing

Go fishing together today! See if you catch anything. Hopefully you will snag wonderful conversation!

90. Saturday: Science

Visit the science museum together. Find a topic that interests your child and research it together!

91. Sunday: Queen/King for the Day 🏛️

Roll out the red carpet or red construction paper today. Declare your child queen or king for the day. Be sure to give him/her a crown from Burger King or you can make one out of paper. Let your child be the boss. He/She can decide what you will play today and what you will eat for each meal. Smile and reply, "Yes, Your Majesty!"

92. Monday: Toasty Beginnings ♥

On a chilly morning, throw your children's clothes in the dryer for a few minutes so they are nice and toasty when put on!

"There are only two lasting bequests we can hope to give our children. One of these is roots; the other, wings."

-Cecilia Lasbury

93. Tuesday: Surprise Coupon 🍽

Reward your child for working extra hard on an assignment by placing a special coupon under his/her dinner plate this evening. It could be redeemable for a half-hour extension on bedtime, a movie for two, or whatever else your little one might adore!

94. Wednesday: Bake a Cake 👄

Use a cake as a greeting card this evening. Create a sweet message that is edible too. You may write, "Great job on your test," "You are brilliant," or "You are the best big brother" on the cake.

95. Thursday: Sweet Awakenings

Wake your child up this morning by playing his/her favorite song!

96. Friday: Labor of Love

Transform your child's chores today. Does your child feed the family pet? Leave a note by the pet dish saying how grateful you are for the wonderful job he/she does caring for the pet. Tape an "I love you" note to the garbage can if your child takes out the trash! People who are appreciated feel valued and loved!

"A child's life is like a piece of paper on which everyone who passes by leaves an impression."

-Chinese Proverb

☐

97. Saturday: Mail Run 📬

A trip to the mailbox can be a very exciting event for a child (especially when that child has a piece of mail addressed directly to him/her!) You can even send a care package filled with play dough so the two of you can play together!

98. Sunday: The Wonka Evening ☺

Tonight snuggle up and watch *Willie Wonka and The Chocolate Factory*. As a surprise, place a "Wonka Bar" on your child's pillow. Prepare the chocolate bar in advance by making your own label and inserting a *golden* ticket. Guaranteed to produce a smile!

99. Monday: Scream for Ice Cream 🍦

When everyone least expects it, declare an ice cream run! Everyone pile into the car and get their favorite treat!

100. Tuesday: Door Knob Recognition ♥

Hang a sign on your child's doorknob recognizing a good deed.

Remember to give children smiles and choices!

"The potential possibilities of any child are the most intriguing and stimulating in all creation."

-Ray L. Wilbur

Conclusion

I hope this book has inspired you to share lots of smiles with your child. Studies have shown that just 15 minutes of playtime a day with a parent produces children who are more creative, have higher self esteem, and exhibit fewer negative behaviors. It is amazing what just a little playtime can do!

"We shall never know all the good that a simple smile can do."
-Mother Teresa

Appendix

<u>Knock-Knock Jokes to tell in the dark:</u>

Knock Knock
Who's there?
Dewey
Dewey who?
Dewey we have to listen to all this knocking?

Knock Knock
Who's there?
Boo
Boo who?
Why are you crying?

Knock Knock
Who's there?
Your mother
Your mother who?
Don't you know your own mother?

Knock Knock
Who's there?
Dwaine
Dwaine who?
Dwaine the bathtub I am drowning!

Knock Knock
Who's there?
Butter
Butter who?
Butter let me in right now or else!

Knock Knock
Who's there?
Noneya
Noneya who?
Noneya business now open the door!

Knock Knock
Who's there?
Amos
Amos who?
A mosquito bit me.

Knock Knock
Who's there?
Andy
Andy who?
And he just bit me again!

Knock Knock
Who's there?
Samoa
Samoa who?
Some more of these bad jokes and I'm out of here!

What sound does a 500-pound canary make?

CHIRP (Yell this as loud as you possibly can!)

Why didn't the skeleton cross the road?

He didn't have the guts!

Quick Idea List

1. Write I love you on the top of your child's hand with an erasable marker!

2. Hang red paper hearts by string in your child's doorway!

3. Create a puzzle by writing a letter to your child on the computer. Highlight the letter and change the font to wingdings. Include one line at the top of the page as a key. To make the key write, "Here is a puzzle for you," in a wingdings font and include a normal font beneath it to serve as a guide to fill in the rest of the puzzle!

4. Use a laundry basket to make a boat, car, or an airplane. Push your child all

around the living room.

5. Place a blanket over the kitchen table. Climb inside the cave!

6. Read this book with your child. Get feedback on the ideas he/she would like to try with you!

7. Show your love with heart shaped food. You can use heart shaped cookie cutters to make grilled cheese sandwiches. You can shape spaghetti noodles like a heart and fill the inside with marinara sauce. You can arrange the pepperoni on a pizza into a heart shape. You can even etch hearts into the butter with a knife! Be as creative as you dare!

8. Play occupation charades. Fill in the

sentence "When I grow up, I want to be…" and act out the different types of jobs. Take turns guessing!

9. Hang a huge welcome home sign inside the front door as an afternoon surprise. Your child will be touched to know that you missed him so much!

Act out an idea right now!

♥ ♥ ♥ ♥ ♥ ♥ ♥ ♥ ♥ ♥ ♥

<u>Ways to Help Improve Fine Motor Skills</u>🖉

By Joyce L. Evans

Complete tasks with child observing which hand he uses. Stop whenever you see frustration. Try another activity or begin again tomorrow.

1. Toothpick construction
2. Lego construction using the small pieces
3. Nail and hammer
4. Nuts and bolts-assemble and take apart
5. Art with finger paint
6. Art with shaving cream
7. Art with pudding
8. Art with seeds
9. Squeeze—balls, lemons, water bottles
10. Wiggle—a rod, drumstick, pencil, through the fingers
try not to drop

✎

11. Sew—needle and thread-sewing cards
12. Straight pin pick up-put into cushion
13. Any games with small pieces to assemble
14. Locks and keys
15. Twisty ties-make a chain, loop or rope
16. String beads
17. Count kernels of popcorn
18. Button
19. Zip
20. Play the piano or keyboard
21. Crack peanuts in shells
22. Play dough

♥ ♥ ♥ ♥ ♥ ♥

Question of the Day:

Ask your child to describe his/her perfect day. More than likely it involves spending time with you. If possible try and create this "perfect" day.

♥ ♥ ♥ ♥ ♥ ♥ ♥ ♥

Things to Ask Your Child

Can you fill in the blank? Double check with your child to make sure your answers are correct.

Favorite color _____
Favorite dinner _____
Favorite dessert _____
Favorite song _____
Favorite movie _____
Favorite friend _____
Favorite thing to do outside

_____

Favorite thing to do inside

_____

Favorite flower _____
Favorite subject at school _____
Favorite book _____
Favorite memory while spending time with
you

Homework Helpers

1. Space Race

If your child does not have a permanently set up spot to do homework, such as a desk in his/her room, this is a good way to start homework time. Use a timer or stopwatch to time how long it takes your child to set up his/her supplies to begin homework. You can even keep track of record times.

Try to create a homework routine. Have a designated homework spot and a designated homework time. It is harder for a child to argue with the clock.

🕐

2. Play Office

Pretend that your child has an office job. He/She can even dress up to look the part. You can be the boss. Tell him/her what they must do at work today (the homework assignments). Then let him/her do the job. If he/she needs a little help, your office is right down the hall.

3. Macaroni Math

Use macaroni to illustrate the concepts of math. They work well for addition, subtraction, division, and even multiplication. The tangible noodles help to make the point.

4. Food Fractions

Pizzas are great helpers when learning fractions; but you can use any food you can cut into equal sized pieces. Just remember to count how many pieces make up the whole.

5. Candy Problems

Turn math into a treat! Simply put an M&M, Skittle, or other favorite candy on each math problem. When your child works exceptionally hard on a problem, he/she gets to eat the candy.

6. More Spelling Fun

While bathing your child this evening, call out your child's spelling list. You can use soap crayons or soap finger-paints. They make a wide array of these products for the bathtub. Simply check your local drugstore.

7. I Write the Songs

Making up songs or rhymes with your child is a fun way to commit things to memory.

8. Alphabet Body Contortion

Let your child practice spelling by forming the letters of the words with his/her body.

9. Map Mosaic

A fun way to learn geography is to make it into a game. Find a map you can cut up. If you have access to the web, factmonster.com/atlas has some good ones. Let your child cut the states apart to make puzzle pieces. Then he/she can put them together.

10. Puppet Play

Playing with puppets can transform the monotony of doing homework. Use the puppets to answer questions, do mental math problems, and recite poems or speeches.

11. Scrabble Scramble

Another way to practice spelling words is to use the tile letters from a scrabble game. You can hand the letters that make up a word to your child and ask him/her to put them together. Or you can ask your child to pick them out without any help. Finally, you can play a game of Scrabble using your child's spelling words.

Index

A

B

P

Q

T

V

W

If you would like to share your ideas or stories on creating smiles in a child's life send them to:

Show Me You Love Me
c/o Beatify Books
P.O. Box 140
Kingmont, WV 26578

Or visit us online at:
Tarakoerber.com

Name			
Address			
City/State		ZIP	
Phone #	E-mail address		
Notice: All prices subject to change without notice			
Title	**Qty**	**Price**	**Total**
Show Me You Love Me		X $9.95	
100 Magical Moments		X $9.95	
		X	

Shipping charges: Please add $2.00 for the first book and $1.00 for each additional book. **Check or money orders only**	Total Qty	Total price
	WV addresses only add appropriate sales tax	Shipping
		Tax
Send to: Orders c/o Beatify Books P.O. Box 140 Kingmont, WV 26578	Total enclosed	